DINOSAUR
Book for Kids

Dinosaur
Book for Kids

Coloring Fun and Awesome Facts

BY KATIE HENRIES-MEISNER

ART BY ANDRE SIBAYAN

Z KIDS · NEW YORK

Published in the United States by Z Kids, an imprint of Zeitgeist™,
a division of Penguin Random House LLC, New York.

zeitgeistpublishing.com

Zeitgeist™ is a trademark of Penguin Random House LLC

ISBN: 9780593196977

Illustrations by Andre Sibayan

Book design by Aimee Fleck

Manufactured in China

6th Printing

To Thalia

Meet the Dinosaurs!

Millions of years ago, a group of reptile-like animals called dinosaurs ruled the planet. They came in all sizes and shapes. Some were as small as chickens and others were bigger than houses! There were carnivores that ate meat, herbivores that ate plants, and omnivores that ate everything. While dinosaurs roamed the earth for a very long time, they are now extinct—they have all died out.

Dinosaurs have been gone from Earth for over 65 million years.

Dinosaurs lived and died long before people showed up on our planet, so how do we know so much about them? Our dinosaur friends left clues behind that can be found today. Paleontologists, the scientists who study dinosaurs, look at fossils—ancient remains of bones, footprints, and other plant or animal parts—to figure out how dinosaurs looked and lived. They have found and studied countless fossils, and discovered more than 500 different types of dinosaurs. Wow!

This fun coloring book

introduces you to 25 awesome dinosaurs. You'll learn how to pronounce their names and find cool facts about each one that you can share with your friends and family. You'll discover what these dinosaurs ate, how big they were, what they looked like, and so much more. Have fun coloring them, learning about them, and becoming a dinosaur expert!

Allosaurus

al-oh-SAWR-us

Carnivore

The **Allosaurus** could lose and regrow its long, sharp teeth, which it needed to eat meat (including other dinosaurs).

Amargasaurus

ah-MAR-guh-SAWR-us

Herbivore

The **Amargasaurus** was smaller than most long-necked dinosaurs and had spines growing from its neck, back, and tail.

Ankylosaurus

an-KIL-oh-SAWR-us

Herbivore

For protection, the **Ankylosaurus** had its own built-in body armor, just like crocodiles today. It also had a heavy club on the end of its tail to bat away anything that tried to hurt it.

Apatosaurus

a-pat-oh-SAWR-us

Herbivore

The **Apatosaurus** was one of the biggest animals to ever live on Earth. Its nostrils, the nose's breathing holes, were on the top of its head.

Archaeopteryx

ar-KEE-OP-ter-icks

Carnivore

The **Archaeopteryx**, a flying dinosaur, helps show us how dinosaurs might have evolved, or changed over time, into the birds we know today. It was about the size of a pigeon and had very strong claws.

Brontosaurus

bron-teh-SAWR-us

Herbivore

The name **Brontosaurus** means "thunder lizard." This long-necked beast would have created ground-shaking thunder with its heavy body as it walked.

Ceratosaurus

ser-RAT-oh-SAWR-us

Carnivore

The name **Ceratosaurus** means "horned lizard," but paleontologists aren't sure how this dinosaur used its nose horn. Some think it may have used the horn to help its babies break out of their eggs.

Corythosaurus

koh-RITH-OH-sawr-us

Herbivore

Scientists know a lot about the **Corythosaurus** because one of its fossils was almost complete and included skin. Along with having a bill like a duck, this dinosaur also had great hearing.

Dilophosaurus

die-LOF-oh-SAWR-us

Carnivore

The **Dilophosaurus** is known for its double-crested head and its ability to run fast on two hind legs. Its big thigh bones helped it run up to 20 miles per hour—almost as fast as an Olympic runner.

Diplodocus

dip-LOD-uh-CUSS

Herbivore

This long-necked and even longer-tailed herbivore may have been the longest dinosaur of all. The **Diplodocus** had two rows of bones under its tail to help balance its huge body.

Giganotosaurus

GEE-gah-NO-toe-SAWR-us

Carnivore

The 6-foot-long head of the **Giganotosaurus** was about the same size as an entire adult human body.

Iguanodon

ig-WHA-nuh-don

Herbivore

This plant-eating dinosaur was happy to graze on all fours, but if a predator came along, the **Iguanodon** could rise up on its two hind legs to run away faster.

Lambeosaurus

LAM-bee-oh-SAWR-us

Herbivore

The **Lambeosaurus** has been called the "hatchet-crested" dinosaur because it had a crest growing from its head that looked like an axe (or hatchet).

Mamenchisaurus

mah-MEN-chee-SAWR-us

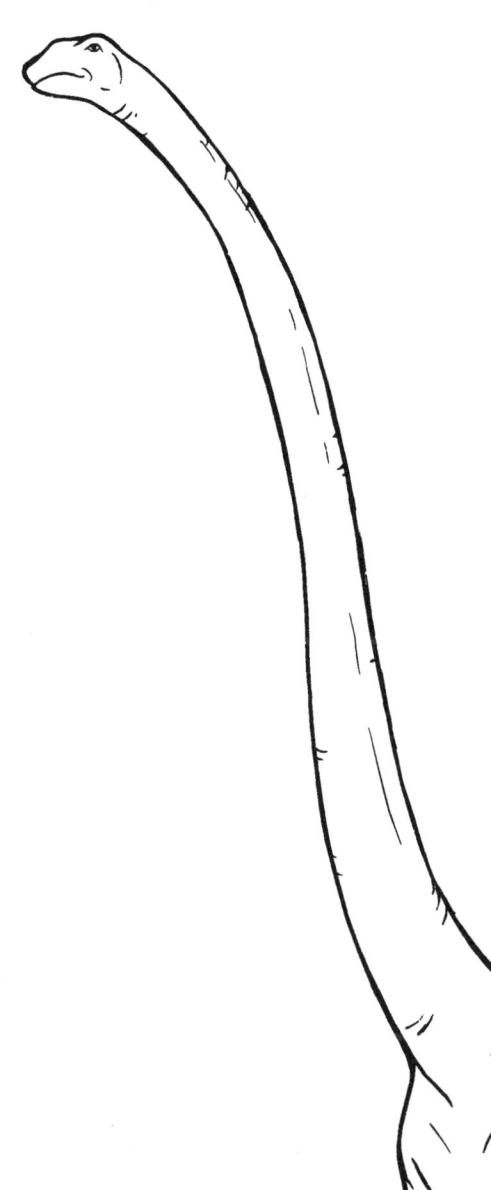

Herbivore

The **Mamenchisaurus** had one of the longest necks of any animal on Earth. Its neck was 46 feet long—the length of a tractor-trailer truck—and held 19 vertebrae, or neck bones, which was more than any other dinosaur.

Ornithomimus

orn-ITH-oh-MY-mus

Omnivore

The **Ornithomimus** looked a lot like an ostrich. It had hollow bones and feathers, just like birds do.

Parasaurolophus

pa-rah-SAWR-OH-luh-fuss

Herbivore

The **Parasaurolophus** had a strangely shaped head with a curved crest that pointed backward. Some paleontologists wonder if this head shape gave it extra-great hearing.

Plateosaurus

PLAT-ee-oh-SAWR-us

Herbivore

The plant-eating **Plateosaurus** had long five-fingered "hands" and weighed 4 times as much as a giant crocodile. It could stand up on its two hind legs to reach its meals.

Protoceratops

pro-toe-SER-rah-tops

Herbivore

The **Protoceratops** was much smaller than its cousins, like the Triceratops. It was about the size of a lion and could weigh close to 400 pounds, thanks to its big, heavy head.

Spinosaurus

SPY-nuh-SAWR-us

Carnivore

With a name meaning "spine lizard," the **Spinosaurus** is famous for the tall "sail" it had growing on its huge back.

Stegosaurus

STEG-uh-SAWR-us

Herbivore

The name **Stegosaurus** means "roofed lizard" because the bony plates on this dinosaur's back created a sort of roof over the giant plant eater.

Styracosaurus

sty-RAK-uh-SAWR-us

Herbivore

The **Styracosaurus** had a total of nine spiky horns growing from its frilled head. No wonder these herbivores have a name that means "spiked lizard"!

Triceratops

try-SER-ah-tops

Herbivore

Triceratops means "3-horned face." This dinosaur had one of the biggest skulls of any land animal ever discovered, which is probably why it could hold up to 800 teeth.

Troodon
TROH-oh-don

Omnivore

Because of the big size of its brain compared to its small body, the **Troodon** is often considered the smartest of all the dinosaurs. This birdlike creature traveled on two legs.

Tyrannosaurus Rex

ty-RAN-uh-sawr-us REX

Carnivore

The **Tyrannosaurus Rex**, or T-Rex, was a meat-eating giant with a huge skull and enormous teeth. The biggest single T-Rex tooth ever found was 12 inches long.

Velociraptor

vel-AH-SER-rap-ter

Carnivore

The **Velociraptor** was a small, super-fast carnivore. It was about the same size as a chicken, probably had feathers, and hunted in groups.

About the Author

Katie Henries-Meisner is a teacher, school leader, and mom of two (dinosaur-loving) kids. She's taught first, third, fourth, fifth, and sixth grades; fourth grade is her favorite! She grew up in suburban Massachusetts, where she developed a passion for urban education and social justice, along with a love of learning through exploration and projects. She currently lives in Northern California with her family.

About the Artist

Andre Sibayan is an illustrator and art director based in the San Francisco Bay Area. He hopes this book will inspire his son, Niko, and children of all ages to be curious about nature and long-ago creatures.